599.3
TIR
SCIENCE CENTER

Tirler, Hermann

A sloth in the family

DATE DUE

MAY 26 '78			
MAY 16 2000			

022677

A Sloth in the Family

A Sloth
in the Family

by
HERMANN TIRLER

translated by
MAURICE MICHAEL

with an Introduction by
GERALD DURRELL

Walker and Company

NEW YORK

Contents

Introduction by Gerald Durrell

The sloth, for some obscure reason, has always been the object of derision. It has probably had more libellous tales told about it than any other mammal, yet it is, as this book will prove, an endearing and enchanting beast.

I became a sloth lover when I went on my first animal collecting expedition to British Guiana. It was not very long before some local hunters procured for me a two-toed sloth, a brownish, rather bear-like creature, whose chief ambition in life was to slash you with his claws—Captain Hook fashion—or else bite you to the bone with a set of remarkably large and very discoloured teeth. Having had my pyjamas ripped open from stem to stern by this animal, I began to feel that sloths were really not the ideal sort of pet, but then I managed to procure a three-toed sloth and instantly it became obvious that, while the two-toed sloth was a misanthropic and irritable type of creature, the three-toed sloth was brimming over with the milk of human kindness and displayed such a benign nature that you had difficulty in believing it was in any way related to the other snorting, savage monster.

One of the three-toed sloth's most endearing qualities was its trustfulness: wild caught, it displayed none of the symptoms of panic that you would expect and lay in my lap smiling up at me with its seductive Mona Lisa-like smile. It accepted food instantly and without hesitation and it accepted also the hut in which I was living. It would trustingly allow me to hang it anywhere and it would then stay in that position, beaming around, until I shifted it to another area of the hut. I was captivated by it and my only regret was that I could not teach it to eat a substitute food and thus get it back to England, so in the end I had to release it.

The flood of misrepresentation that this charming animal has been subjected to in literature is quite extraordinary. Here, for example, is what one Gonzalo Ferdinando de Oviedo said about it:

'There is,' he writes, 'another beast, which, by a name of contrary effect, the Spaniards call "cagnuolo", that is, the light dogge, whereas it is one of the slowest beasts in the world, and so heavie and dull in moving, that it can scarcely goe fiftie pases in a whole day: these beasts are in the same land, and are very strange to behold for the disproportion that they have to all other beasts: they are about two spans in length when they are growne to their full bignesse, but when they are very young, they are somewhat more grosse then long: they have foure subtill feete, and in every one of them foure clawes like unto birds, and joyned together: yet are neither their clawes or their feet able to susteine their bodies from the ground, by reason whereof, and by the heavinesse of their bodies, they draw their bellies on the ground: their neckes are high and streight, and all equal like the pestle of a mortar, which is altogether equal even unto the top, without making any proportion or similitude of a head, or any difference except in the noddle, and in the tops of their neckes: they have very round faces much like unto owles, and have a marke of their own haire after the manner of a circle, which maketh their faces seeme somwhat more long then large: they have small eyes and round, and nostrils like unto monkeyes: they have little mouthes, and moove their neckes from one side to another, as though they were astonished.'

The sloth might well be astonished at reading this.

Why people got the impression that a sloth could barely stir himself into sufficient activity to walk fifty paces in a day is extraordinary because anyone who has watched a sloth will know that it is capable of quite a considerable turn of speed through the branches if it feels so inclined.

Not content with this, Señor Ferdinando de Oviedo continues by saying that—

'And whereas I my selfe have kept them in my house, I could never perceive other but that they live onely of aire: and of the same opinion are in like manner all men of those regions, because they have never seene them eate any thing, but ever turne their heads and mouthes toward that part where the wind bloweth most, whereby may be considered that they take most pleasure in the ayre.'

It seems to me extraordinary that even in those days of unnatural history, anyone could keep a sloth for any length of time without perceiving it feeding on leaves.

Another early traveller, Joseph Acosta, was a little more accurate in his description, but he also fell down when it came to describing the sloth's diet:

'There is another strange beast, which for his great heavinesse, and slownesse in moving, they call "perico-ligero", or the little light dogge; hee hath three nailes to every hand, and mooves both hand and feete, as it were by compasse and very heavily: it is in face like to a monkey, and hath a shrill crie; it climeth trees and eates ants.'

The famous Buffon, in his Natural History, left no stone unturned in his effort to blacken the sloth's character and ended his diatribe on it with the words that it had 'a strange and bungling conformation of features to whom nature has been unkind, and who exhibit to us the picture of innate misery.' Anyone glancing through the photographs in this book would be able to correct Buffon of that statement.

Apart from their extraordinary adaptation to an arboreal life, sloths exhibit other curious characteristics. They are in many ways more like reptiles than mammals. They have the most imperfect control over their body temperatures and can easily die of cold, simply because they cannot adjust their temperature with the rapidity of a normal mammal. Again they are capable of surviving large doses of poison which would kill any other animal of a similar size and even surviving the most ghastly wounds which would carry off a less stoical creature.

One naturalist describes how a sloth was brought in to him and he kept it for several days. It seemed happy and contented and fed well. Then one day he noticed that it was scratching at the hair on its stomach with its claws. A close investigation revealed that it had in fact got a hole in it the size of a half-crown, caused by an enormous lump of lead. The creature had been shot at and the lead ball had penetrated right through into its internal organs. A lesser creature would have died from this wound, but the sloth appeared to be completely oblivious of it.

Those of you who are getting tired of books about lions or tigers and other such animals should welcome this one with open arms: firstly because of its amusing illustrations, and secondly because at long last somebody has had the courage to strike a blow on behalf of this fascinating and much maligned creature.

I

How we Acquired our Sloth

For years my wife had had a thing about sloths. She felt that the jungly garden of our house on the outskirts of Rio de Janeiro would not be complete without a sloth and I promised to get her one. But I am an engineer, not a naturalist and did not know how to set about fulfilling my promise.

Sloths are rare and not a great deal is known about them, so I went to the library in search of facts and found myself reading an ancient tome bound in pigskin: *Tractates of Hairie Beasties*. This provided me with a lot of irrelevant information. Of the sloth it said: '. . . this wight is so abominably sluggish that to get from one tree to another, he doth squander twain whole days, and on that count hathe forever to bear the name of Lazy Sloth.' This encouraged me because obviously, once found, my sloth was not going to be difficult to catch. In more modern books I learned other facts about the sloth.

These animals are related to the armadillo and to the ant-eater. The official name of the three-toed sloth is *bradypus tridactylus*, which means three-fingered, a much better description than three-toed, because the three claws on his front paws are good serviceable fingers. His cousin, the *choloepus* (two-toed sloth) has two toes and two 'fingers'. Sloths are classed as *edentates*, which means that they have no front teeth. One might suppose that this would make it difficult for them to eat but, in fact, it is a very practical device for the easy insertion of the finger-shaped fruit of the ymbahuba, the sloth's favourite food.

If he sometimes appears rather like a spectral being out of the nebulous past, that is as it should be: this is exactly what he is. Sloths are descendants of a family once numerous and comprising many species, one of which was the hippo-sized *megatherium*.

The three-toed sloth has other curiosities: its gullet and windpipe are abnormally, astonishingly, long and allow its head to revolve without discomfort or inconvenience in eating and breathing. It has an unusually large number of vertebrae, one or two floating ribs and a heart that is unusually small in relation to its size.

Some time later my work took me into the Itatiaya Mountains and there, one day, I saw a sapling behaving in a strange way: for no apparent reason it slowly bent over and down until the top was touching the ground, though none of its neighbours moved. Investigation showed that there was a sloth at the top of the sapling. It must have gone there to feed on the tender shoots and had frozen, hoping not to be seen, when I appeared on the scene but by bad luck it was too heavy for the tree-top. Rather cautiously I took hold of the animal and tried to pick it off, but it clung to its refuge. I tugged and pulled, but the sloth would not let go. I did not know what to do; but having at last found a sloth, I was determined not to let it go. In the end I took my big machete and severed the trunk, then I shouldered the tree-top complete with sloth and bore them away rejoicing.

In repose, a permanently good-natured smile

In our tropical garden, where conditions are not very different to those in the real jungle *(opposite)*, Nepomuk angles for a young tree, too slender to bear his weight

The finger-shaped fruit of the ymbahuba tree

A sloth holds on to the stalk of the fruit he is eating, when fed by hand
the human arm becomes the 'stalk' with painful consequences

Nepomuk is overcome by sleep while hanging from a mulungu tree

When the eyes are shut, the dark eye-stripes show up strongly, giving
the A-i an intimidating look

Nepomuk using his sharp and very strong claws to climb a Ravenala palm

When I got home, since we had no sloth-house, the beast was put into the bathroom where we left it for a couple of hours to recover and to get used to its new surroundings. When we returned, we found our sloth sitting in the washhand basin, the taps were running, water was spilling over on to the floor and all our towels had been pulled off the rails. The floor was covered with excrement and awash, the walls were splashed and dirty, and the poor little sloth looked bewildered and forlorn and was dripping wet.

Such was our rather unhappy introduction to life with a sloth. But we soon discovered what an endearing creature it was: it was peace-loving and quiet and, except when shut up where it shouldn't be, clean. Its small honest eyes looked you straight in the face, unless or until their tired lids sank slowly over them, as often happened, for the sloth needed fifteen hours' sleep a day. It had a great variety of expression. When its face was in repose a good-natured smile was forever on its lips.

Sloths never bite, all their movements are incredibly slow and they never make a sound, except on very rare occasions, when they heave a gentle sigh that sounds like *a-i*—hence the Brazilians call them a-i. Sloths are so human in appearance—and in some of their ways—that inevitably one tends to judge them by human standards.

The a-i is shy and retiring; it is also gentle and patient and looks so appealingly helpless that it is hard to resist the temptation to pick it up and cuddle it. But, of course, no wild animal, even the gentlest, will allow one to take such liberties until it knows one very well. Each of our a-i's muscular arms and legs was equipped with three large claws for climbing, in an emergency they could also be used as weapons. A young sloth has sharp claws; our a-i was young and its claws were very sharp indeed, and this is what had enabled it to climb the vertical tiled bathroom wall. It had used the grooves between the tiles to reach the basin and then, no doubt clawing frantically in search of a hold, had inadvertently turned on the taps.

We were relieved to find that the sloth would eat from our hands; it was only interested in two kinds of food; ymbahuba or ficus.

The ymbahuba (*cecropia lyratilobe*) is an exotic, tall, strangely shaped tree with long bare arms, which have green or silvery fan-shaped clusters of leaves at their ends. While high up, at the crest, hang bunches of red fruit with a wonderfully strong scent. These are known locally as *mão-de-macaco*, because in shape they resemble the paw of a monkey.

We had a little shed-cum-summerhouse in the grounds; which we now cleared and turned into a sloth-house. We put two trees inside it, so that the sloth should have something to climb and also two shallow boxes, one filled with sand and the other with dead leaves, they were intended to fulfil the purpose of the cinder tray with which cats are provided. Though sloths are supposed to be slow in the uptake, ours caught on to the idea at once and during the two months he spent in the house, always made use of them. He must have approved of his house for he showed no signs of claustrophobia nor did he make any attempt to get out. We cut two holes in the door through which we could observe him. After two months we felt that he had settled down, so we gave him the freedom of the garden with its sixty trees and high surrounding wall.

By now it was time to give him a name. As there was something about his face that reminded me of the statue of St Nepomuk in Prague (Nepomuk was a priest who was thrown into the Moldau River by King Wenceslas because he would not give away information obtained in the confessional) we called him Nepomuk.

We wanted to tame him and to accustom him to being handled and soon discovered that the best technique was to stalk him from behind and grab him by the scruff. Sloths hit out but cannot reach behind themselves, in any case there is no difficulty in escaping the blow aimed at you, for even when in a temper, the a-i behaves with the utmost deliberation. Slowly and solemnly he swings an arm up as he gives a single snort of indignation, then there is a long pause and it is only after this that down come his claws.

During the first days he spent with us, Nepomuk occasionally hit out, but once he had accepted us and had grown accustomed to his new surroundings, he never again aimed a blow at us. He trusted us and became absolutely reliable. Nevertheless we still had to be careful, because now he seemed to regard us as trees and was inclined to dig his claw into our 'bark' and this was excessively painful. On the other hand he could not bite since he had no teeth in the requisite place.

Feeding our quiet, unobtrusive guest presented no problem in our tropical climate, his food was to be had for the taking in the bush and jungle round our house for all he required for his well-being was ymbahubas and more ymbahubas. Sloths spend most of their lives in these trees, feeding on their juicy leaves, blossom and fruit. They never build a nest or shelter but sleep exposed to all weathers curled up in the fork of a branch.

Often they could be mistaken for a wasp's or tree-termite's nest. The Karaja Indians have a story about sloths and their lack of shelter.

Tomorrow the Sloths will build Nests

It was night in the forest and raining most terribly. The storm lashed at the branches on which the a-is slept unprotected. The rain poured off them; the mothers were shivering and the babies crying. Then a father sloth remarked: 'Tomorrow we'll build nests!' 'Yes, tomorrow, without fail,' another agreed.

Next day, they had breakfast, to wake them up, then they enjoyed a good bask in the sun, to dry off; after this they had a little snooze, to gather strength, and by then they felt so well that nobody thought any more about building nests. At least not until another terrible downpour fell and another storm lashed at the branches on which the a-is were sleeping quite unprotected. The rain poured off them, the mothers were shivering and their babies crying.

And the fathers? Unanimously the father sloths decided: 'Tomorrow we'll build nests.'

II

Eating and Sleeping

As I said, a-is delight in ymbahuba shoots. Though they also appreciate matapan buds and the silky translucent pink leaves of the cacao, ymbahuba is their favourite food. Unfortunately, young ymbahuba trees are too slender to climb, but the a-i does not let himself be put off by that. He climbs an adjacent, stouter tree and from there angles for the ymbahuba. If *one* arm is not enough, he will use both, and when he does so he looks like a flag flying from its halyard. This acrobatic feat, performed in slow-motion, calls for considerable strength, but the sloth is an athlete. He is also something of a rubber man, and has a sickening habit of turning his head round and round, until you are sure his neck is going to snap off. But it doesn't for, short though it is, it has more vertebrae in it than a giraffe's and is extremely flexible.

Sloths belong to the family of *xenarthra*, and have that family's peculiar accessory articulations in the last pectoral and lumbar vertebrae; this double-jointedness allows them to perform the most gruesome looking acrobatics. Not only can they turn their necks through four hundred degrees but also, while hanging by a leg, can turn their bodies through almost three hundred and sixty degrees. When we first saw Nepomuk doing this our blood ran cold and we felt sure the limb must be torn right off. It was a horrible performance to watch but in the end we got quite used to it. We also learned that a sloth is a tough animal, and that an occasional fall from a tree doesn't hurt it.

I soon realised how right my wife had been to wish to have a sloth in the family for the very sight of one makes you smile. Its stubbly chin might be that of a good-natured, rather unkempt hermit; its mouth that of a person well-pleased with himself and the world. Its myopic eyes are brown and have tiny pupils that are almost invisible by day and only one eighth of an inch in diameter when adjusted to complete darkness. Its ears are hidden beneath a fringe of hair like that of a tonsured monk, on the whole it does not hear well, yet there are certain sounds to which it is sensitive and reacts swiftly, for any one of these noises may indicate the presence of an enemy:

The snap of a twig in the undergrowth—a jaguar?
a whistle in the air—a harpy eagle?
a rustle among the leaves—a giant snake?

At any of these sounds, the poor a-i will shrink in terror and, if it should happen to see anything resembling one of these predators, it will almost fall off its branch with fright. Once, after Nepomuk had withdrawn to a mulungu tree for the evening and was dozing pleasantly, he was awakened by the slithering rustle of a giant snake just below him, in fact he actually saw his enemy creeping along (incidentally, it was following me). Nepomuk hid among the leaves and, luckily, as dusk was falling, the snake never noticed the quaking sloth above it. It was an immensely long reptile and had a yellow head from which water suddenly spurted out over the bushes; I killed it and put it into the shed. Nepomuk saw this happen and it seemed that the episode was altogether too much for him for he hid his head in his arms and stayed like that for a long time.

When he recovered he went to sleep among the flame-red flowers of a coral tree and all we could see was a soft ball of fur, so still that it was difficult to observe the slow silent movement of his breathing. Even the small but powerful stumpy tail that, in the daytime, was such a useful climbing aid was now laid flat, helping to round off the sleeping ball.

On another occasion when Nepomuk had fallen asleep embracing the trunk of a tree with his arms and legs, I was able to go up and examine his fur. His pelt con-sisted of two layers: a trim, white fluff that acted as waterproof underclothes and a longer thick coat of a darker colour. There was no parting down the back but one on the belly. As a result, when an a-i has hung himself up on a branch waiting for better weather, the rain runs off him. The male sloth's fur looks either grey or browny, depending on the light, and is patterned with white and he has a yellow patch on his back. The females and the young have much plainer coats.

Apart from its colouring, which imitates that of the ymbahuba tree and provides excellent camouflage, nature has given the a-i another means of passive defence. When resting during the day, at which time his head will not be tucked in, the sloth instead of wearing his normal, friendly expression appears quite intimidating, for his black eye-stripes look like gigantic menacing eyes. A jaguar would probably not be taken in by this, but the semi-wild cats that hunt in the jungle beyond our

23

garden are, and they scamper away when they see Nepomuk.

The striking markings on the a-i's head also serve as visual signals. When searching for a mate, the male sloth cannot follow the trail of the female in season as animals which live on the ground do: he has to look for these black stripes beneath the white of the forehead. The female helps him in his search by emitting loud bird-like cries of *eee* or *a-eee* at intervals as regular as a minute gun. The approach of the male is slow and deliberate and silent. He does not reply to her calls. When he reaches her, the female raises her tail and is mated from behind.

Sloths sleep a lot, eat little and drink not at all; so it is no wonder that it is sometimes weeks before they make a puddle. (Black dry pellets appear more frequently.) They have a very low metabolic rate and consequently a slow rate of growth and in the natural state, if they do not fall victim to a predator, are likely to live to a ripe old age. Food and sleep are almost their only preoccupations with the accent perhaps on sleep. When asleep they remain totally motionless; I tested this by putting a plastic disc (it was heavy enough not to be dislodged by the wind, but only by movement) on Nepomuk's head one evening after he had fallen asleep, and I found it still there in the morning. The same experiment has been carried out with wild sloths in the jungle. There have been times when Nepomuk seemed unable to rouse himself even for food; yet, if one gently pushed a leaf between his lips, having once started to eat, he would go on and on. His fast was only due to his inability to make up his mind to start eating. The Indians have a story which explains why the sloth doesn't drink.

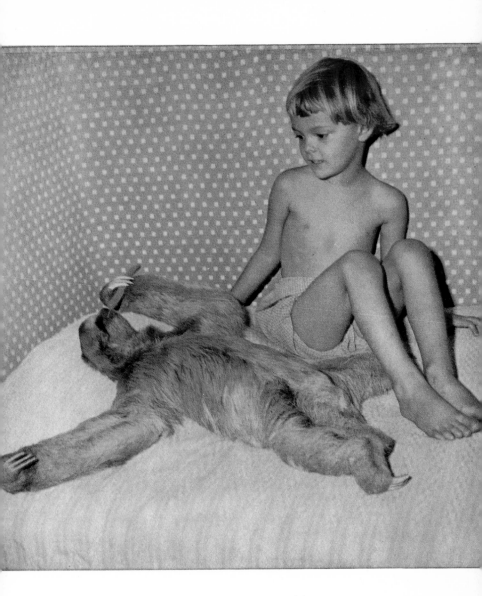

Sloths will eat in any position

After a storm, Nepomuk comes down from his tree in search of food
and comfort, but is hung up to dry before allowed into the house

On the ground, the adult sloth is almost helpless

I could never make out whether Nepomuk liked music or was trying
to make me stop

A sleeping sloth can look remarkably like a wasp's nest

Nepomuk's wife soon after capture, ready to hit out at anyone who
approached

Sloths are surprisingly fast and determined swimmers

Why the a-i smiles and never drinks

In the old days, long long ago, the a-i was a thoroughly nasty animal. He rushed about through the forest, annoying everyone with his hurry and greed. One day, the god Merekelu decided to come down to earth once more. He waited for four times seven days until the window of the moon again stood wide open,[1] and then let himself down on a liana. Landing in the Sapucaya Forest he went to a water-hole to refresh himself. Respectfully the tapir and the golden hare, the jaguar, the ant-bear and all the animals, drew aside to let him drink first, not so the a-i, which thrust in front of him and drank and drank as though it would never stop. This made Merekelu angry and he told a-i that he was going to cast a spell upon him to punish him. A-i was terrified and expected to be killed, but Merekelu just breathed over him, extinguishing for ever all the hurry and thirst in him. Greatly relieved, for he had expected much worse, a-i smiled to himself, but from that moment he has never drunk again and has been the easy-going fellow we know.

Before each meal, Nepomuk—who is a gourmet—will give his lips one soft smack of relish and then begin to eat neatly. From then on, he will devote himself to this important task with such single-mindedness that

[1]To the Bororo Indians the moon is not an object in the sky illuminated by the sun, but a hole in the black velvet of the heavens: a window that opens and shuts and through which can sometimes be seen the bright world of the spirits.

nothing will distract him from it except the need to sleep. We never saw him lick his coat; he must have relied on heavy tropical showers to keep him clean. He only put out his tongue as a sign of distaste—if, for instance, there was something wrong with the leaf he was eating.

Every day Nepomuk eats three or four big leaves and one or two flowers. He will eat in every conceivable and inconceivable position, sitting, lying, even hanging head downwards, sometimes he may even be overcome by sleep when upside down, but usually he sleeps sitting in a branch, curled into a furry ball with his head tucked in or lying flat on his back with his head resting on one of his arms. This is the position he usually adopts when he goes to one of our bedrooms for a siesta after Sunday lunch. He climbs on to a bed and makes himself comfortable, after which we sometimes hear a scarcely audible grumbling sound that is obviously a sign of contentment. At first we thought he might be purring but later discovered that it was caused by a gentle grinding of his teeth. When he wakes he makes his slow laborious way—if he doesn't insist on being carried— back to his world of trees.

Nepomuk always has the freedom of the house and on Sundays he has lunch with us; his meal consists of the tastiest leaves and buds we can find, followed by macaco.

When eating, the a-i holds on to its food, which is of course normally growing on a tree, but when it is being fed on the ground, its claws, which are designed for climbing, are too awkward to hold detached fruit properly and convey it to his mouth, the result is that the sloth frequently loses both his food and his balance.

26

Because of this we have always been careful to hold on to any fruit that we are giving Nepomuk and allow him to cling to our fingers. The clinging claws have the action and occasion the pain of a thumbscrew, yet our doting children vie with each other to be allowed to feed their dear a-i.

Not infrequently, while we are sitting at supper, someone will raise the alarm: 'Sloth burning!' at which we leap to our feet and run frantically round trying to discover where Nepomuk has fallen asleep. On the kitchen stove? No! On the water heater in the bath-room? No! There he is on top of the floor lamp in the drawing-room, with his bottom touching the big electric bulb!

Poor fellow, he cannot understand why his smoking backside is hurting, for to associate the bulb under his behind with the cause of his suffering is evidently beyond his intellectual capacity, so he just sits stubbornly on. We struggle to get him down, but he clings desperately to his perch, refusing to budge and protesting with many *ah-eees* against our unwarranted disturbance of his slumbers. For days after this, those of our visitors who are zoologically-minded never fail to notice the brown patch on our a-i's behind. Is ours a new species, we are asked? No, just the brand of a hundred-watt bulb.

The fruit of the ymbahuba has a scent like a hyacinth's and this clings to our fingers; attracted by it, Nepomuk often reaches out to an empy hand and tries to eat it and not till his dry, leathery snub-nose touches our fingers, does he discover his mistake and even then he remains incredulous.

Once I thought I would see just how long Nepomuk could go on eating and provided myself with a large store of his favourite foods. He hung on to my left arm, and I pushed blossom into his mouth till he was quite white with pollen and began to sneeze. Whenever he closed his eyes and was on the point of dropping off I gave him an encouraging pat on his behind which made the pollen fly and set him off eating again, slowly but surely. Finally, he became so sleepy that, in order not to fall off, he took such a firm grip of my 'branch' that I screamed with pain and had to shout for my wife to help to release me. After that we bundled Nepomuk unceremoniously into a tree.

The *bradypus*, three-toed sloth, is not the least interested in our human foods. Its tastes are most conservative. I knew of a Brazilian who fed two of them on rice and beans, the staple diet of the poor in Brazil: both died. The two-toed sloth is not so fastidious and might have survived on that diet.

Everything about a sloth appears agreeably spherical, but if you feel it, you will discover that this appearance is due to its fur and that the animal's body is thin and made up entirely of bone and muscle.

People are seldom tempted to hunt sloths and if they do the a-i usually contrives to escape, so not many sloth-skin saddlecloths are to be seen or sloth-claws made into Indian necklaces. One reason for this is that if you shoot an a-i which is up in a tree, you will seldom get it, because in death it will remain clinging to its branch and few people are prepared to climb a hundred-and-fifty foot jungle giant just to retrieve a sloth. The Indians, however, have developed a device to overcome this problem; it is an arrow with a heavy knob of clay at the end. This, if aimed correctly, can stun the a-i and bring it tumbling down alive.

Should you be near enough—and unkind enough—to tickle a sleeping sloth with a stick, you will call his wrath down upon yourself—in as far as one can speak of so violent an emotion in connection with this gentle creature. First, a sleepy head will emerge from its hollow and look down to locate the cause of the disturbance. Not seeing one, yet feeling that it is better to be safe than sorry, the a-i will start up the mechanism that in due course will send a swinging blow sweeping through the air beneath him. Then, exhausted by the effort, he will doze off again. But the insult will rankle and, an hour later, half asleep and eyes tight shut, he will still be muttering to himself and every now and again hitting out at the empty air below his perch— just in case his assailant should still be there.

Should you want your sloth and discover that he is hidden in the leafy crest of a tree, you must call for him in a friendly, monotonous tone, again and again and again. Eventually, a head will appear high above you and peer down. But it will be some time before a-i can make up his mind to descend, for he is no advocate of precipitate action.

III

A Garden for Sloths

Our tropical garden is brilliant with blossom all the year round, but in December, which is the beginning of the Brazilian summer, the blaze of colour is magnificent. There is the cerulean of the palisander flowers, the purple of the mulungu blossom, the yellow of the cassia bushes and everywhere the pink of a creeper known here as 'Love's Embrace'. Then too our yucca palms seem to be dripping with white blossom and the humming birds and bees, perhaps attracted by the scent, swarm in them.

Night is a lovely time in the garden for the darkness is filled with whisperings and whistlings and strange little noises; it smells of damp earth, decay and orchids, and the air is alive with the rhythmic dance of luminous insects. Now and again an urutau makes a sound which may be a love call or a death cry—I have never been able to discover which. When morning comes and the sunlight wakes the silvery butterflies to life among the red hibiscus and yellow bemtevi, birds come flying in to feed on the yhvapuru trees whose shiny black berries cling close to their trunks in such profusion as almost to cover them. Golden-green iridescent humming birds preen among the sapphire luxuriance of the jacarandas and, as the sun rises higher, the cicadas begin

their sizz-sizz-sizzle concert and the flowers unfold in
their thousands.

Ours is an Eden of a garden and so far as Nepomuk
is concerned there are hardly any restrictions but what is
all this compared to the splendid freedom of the jungle-
clad mountains where he spent his youth? Remember-
ing this we feel that his attachment to us is a gift and it
touches us. Does he like us only because we feed him?
Surely not for he will come down to us out of the trees
that are covered with delicious buds. On the other hand,
it must be admitted that he has discovered that a human
lap makes a softer and warmer seat than a tree, and that
sleep is twice as sweet if your head is being scratched.
Anyway, the fact that our a-i likes our company, what-
ever the reason, gives us a lot of pleasure.

There is a tree in our garden which humming birds,
called 'flower-kissers' in Brazil, delight in. One day,
when Nepomuk was up this tree, a humming bird flew
close and then hung there in the air with thrumming
wings observing the sloth. Suddenly there was a loud
crack among the branches, the humming bird darted
away and poor Nepomuk tumbled out of the tree and
landed with a thud on the ground, where he sat gazing
round him with a look of amazement on his face.

What had happened was this: when climbing, a sloth
often gropes blindly; his claws seize on to anything
within reach, in a strong and lightning reflex action
regardless of what the object may be, on this occasion
it was his own tail, so no wonder he lost his balance.

In spite of such accidents it is usually a pleasant sight
to watch a sloth climbing for its slow, deliberate movements are very graceful. On the ground, the poor a-i
is in a very different case, for then he becomes a helpless

creature unable even to raise himself up. To move, he has to stretch out his forelegs and pull himself along laboriously, digging his claws into the ground. His short hind legs do what they can to help, but that is not much and the sloth's belly never clears the ground. In sandy soil he leaves a most peculiar track. On the polished floors in our house, Nepomuk is prone and helpless.

Is it true, as the old book I read said, that he 'doth squander twain whole days' to get from one tree to another? Certainly not, because sloths seldom come down to the ground to cross from one tree to another.

When a storm goes roaring through the forest, it is Nepomuk's delight to take to the tree-tops, where he gives a display of breath-taking acrobatics. Climbing to the topmost branch, he will let his weight pull him into a horizontal position, pointing towards the neighbouring tree; then, cautiously distributing his weight between a number of twigs, he will edge his way to the very end, and, while the rain pours off him and the wind jerks him this way and that, he will make a long arm at the next tree-top as it swings towards him and away again; then, as it returns on the next gust, things happen in a rush: Nepomuk catches hold of a twig of the swaying crest, then swiftly seizes another two; but often they are obviously far too weak to climb on to and already the tree-top is swinging back. At this point, if I am watching the proceedings, my heart leaps into my mouth as I see Nepomuk crash into the foliage of the next tree. But I need not worry for there he hangs, unperturbed, swaying to and fro until he finally comes to rest.

These storms are the only things that ever cause Nepomuk to become restless when he is indoors, for

Nepomuk's 'fingers' command respect

A favourite position for sleep is in the fork of a branch, Nepomuk and his wife tuck in their heads and curl themselves into two furry balls

The male sloth's fur is patterned with white and has a yellowish marking
on the back

Like a flag flying from its halyard, Nepomuk swings both arms to reach his objective

As soon as the baby sloth began to suckle, the mother would eat nothing
but the juicy top shoots of the young ymbahuba

Our eldest daughter with Nepomuk

to him, a storm means waving tree-tops, crests touching each other and the possibility of easy tree-top travel.

When he has been out in a storm, after it is all over and the rain has stopped, he will usually come down from the trees in search of food and creature comforts and make for our home, but a wet sloth is something my wife will not have in the house. So she picks him up and hooks him up on the washing line along with the clothes she has just put out to dry, and there he hangs among the flapping washing and seems to enjoy it. Before long the warmth of the sunlight will make him sleepy and he will doze off, but before he reaches that stage, there will be a great deal of snorting and sneezing, because the water that runs down his body keeps getting into his nose.

The airy crests of the ymbahuba and mulungu trees offer little protection against the scorching midday sun, but there are other trees with thicker foliage, in whose cool recesses a sloth can enjoy a siesta. Mimosa, orchids and ferns also provide a wonderful hide-out. Sometimes when setting up my ladder and camera I disturbed Nepomuk but, when he sees who it is, he just snorts and doesn't move. After I have taken my photos, peace returns except for the distant bell-like call of the araponga, the melancholy sweet high notes of the sahy and the montonous concert of buzzing and humming insects. Then Nepomuk yawns hugely, rolls up and relapses into sleep.

Ymbahuba trees, which are the natural home of the a-i, seldom grow in marshy ground or even near water, so it is not often that a sloth has to swim. Yet, though water is certainly not his element, he is an adept swimmer when the need arises. His fur, which is unusually thick, keeps the water out and is so full of air that it makes him buoyant, so he has little difficulty in keeping himself afloat. He swims along, his arms working strongly and his behind waggling elegantly. Gone are his sluggishness and sloth. Slow on land, Nepomuk is surprisingly quick and determined in the water, but I do not know whether this is because he likes it or because he is filled with an urgent desire to get out of it as quickly as possible. Certainly water has one disadvantage: he cannot stop in it for a snooze. I believe, therefore, that he never goes in deliberately but just enters water when it happens to be in his path.

Slowness of movement, good camouflage and the fact that he makes no sound, all help to prevent the sloth from being discovered by its enemies; moreover they never know where to look for him since he has no home. No doubt it is for these reasons that the gentle a-i has been able to survive through the ages while other species, better equipped to defend themselves, have died out.

Sloths were not always small animals but all that remains of the prehistoric giant sloth are some fossilized skeletons; they are almost the size of an elephant. All have been found in the American continent and, after testing them with their radio-isotopes and pollen analysis, scientists say they date back to the Tertiary period. Judging by its build and strong jaws, the giant sloth was neither so slow nor so gentle as our a-is are; and it cannot, presumably, have understood the art of hiding as well as ours do; since, despite its pugnacity, it has long been extinct.

The somnolent a-i of today, who detests nothing so much as quarrelling, has retained little of the ferocity of his primeval ancestors; if you try to provoke him, which, especially when he gives you one of his disarmingly trusting looks you won't want to do, his only reaction will be to draw in his breath, as though surprised that anyone could be so cantankerous. After which, exhausted by this emotional storm, he will subside into a deep sleep.

IV

Nepomuk gets Married

The characteristic slowness of today's sloths is only conditional: when they have to fight or take to flight, they can be fast movers. We discovered this when we introduced Nepomuk's intended bride to him. She was young and most energetic.

She had been caught in the forest at Silvestre, a mile or two outside Rio, where the negroes go at night to hold their secret, ghost-exorcising rites. On these occasions the throb of muffled drums reverberates through the forest, and flaring torches cast an eerie gleam over the rocks and tropical vegetation. Terrified by the noise and the flames, all the animals in the vicinity take flight. This young sloth must have gone in the wrong direction and so was caught, and her captors brought her to us.

When I captured Nepomuk he just clung stubbornly to his tree-top and only vented his indignation in a brief, but distinct, *ah-eee* but this young female hit out wildly, snorted and made furious attempts to get at her enemies. I was concerned for Nepomuk who, though well-mannered and dignified, is emotional, and I was afraid that he might be put off by such a display of female temperament.

The first meeting did not pass off altogether smoothly, though it did not come up to my worst expectations.

When Nepomuk caught sight of the stranger he began, without undue haste, to climb the tree in which she was sitting. Apparently the lady wanted the tree to herself, for when he came within reach, he was greeted with a resounding blow on his head. After a pause for consideration, Nepomuk climbed down again but was followed by the female who rained a shower of cuffs and blows upon him. Then abruptly she changed her tactics and began making inviting advances. This was altogether too sudden for poor Nepomuk, who took fright and, turning, with a hasty *ah-eee* by way of good-bye, fled in panic. Knocking his intended bride over in his flight, he hid in the bushes.

Throughout the day, he remained in a state of great agitation, climbing with unsuspected speed and agility from tree to tree. Indeed he seemed so upset that we removed the female so as to allow him time to accustom himself to the prospect of getting married.

Full of feminine charm as our new a-i was, her behaviour was deplorable and when I went to inspect her at closer quarters, I was able to appreciate the horror she had inspired in her future husband; for no sooner had I come within a respectful distance of the branch which she was jealously guarding, than she gave a snort of defiance, let herself drop till she was hanging by one hind-leg and struck out with both arms. The blow was amazingly well-aimed and savage. I withdrew, scratched and bleeding, regretting the old days when Nepomuk's ceremonial threatening gesture gave one notice of an impending blow and ample time to get out of its range. Now, I recognised that our female sloth was certainly no beauty with her threatening eyes, slapping claws and patchy fur, but this did not seem a sufficient reason to cause Nepomuk, who was strong, to flee in horror, instead of defending himself. I knew that an animal that has been with people since it was a baby often regards itself as being of the same species, and I began to wonder whether our a-i had become unable to recognise a fellow-sloth when he saw one.

We decided to keep the two apart for a while; in the meantime we tried with the help of good food, soothing words and cautious stroking to convince the new arrival that she was not surrounded by dangers, but by love and care. Only if we could gain her trust would we again attempt to bring the two together. We were most anxious that they should like each other, for how else could we hope for a baby a-i?

In fact, it was not long before the young a-i's ever-growing appetite showed that she had accepted her new surroundings and was feeling more or less at home. But though she accepted us she did not, as yet, accept Nepomuk. It was only after we stopped hearing them making *ah-ees* (an expression of misery and despair on his part and on hers a war-cry) that we felt things were looking up. She was still liable to pull Nepomuk's hair out by the fistful, but at least she no longer hit him, which was an improvement. She would still draw her arm back as though to strike, but now we often found her asleep in this attitude, somnolence having obviously overcome her before she could carry out her threat; even asleep, she would sometimes growl and look terrifying, but we were no longer to be intimidated, for by now we knew that in the world of the sloths, sleep is always mightier than the claw.

Eventually her treatment of Nepomuk improved, indeed her behaviour towards him now entitled him to be called her suitor. They still had squabbles. Sometimes these were related to food, for the lady was extremely greedy and was once so carried away that she snatched a leaf from Nepomuk's mouth. It must have been an especially delicious one, for he protested—and got his hair pulled for his pains! Kindness and care will transform almost any creature of the wilds into a friend and this is particularly true of young animals.

But the taming of the shrew took a full four weeks. By then it dawned upon her that Nepomuk was not her enemy, and she realised that we, too, meant her well.

Violent and crotchety as this young sloth had at first been, she became sweet and gentle. Within a month of ceasing to be restless and moody, she grew to be fat and complacent, and from never sleeping more than twelve hours a day, she slept up to eighteen. Her coat, that had been staring and dull, became smooth and glossy and we began to feel that soon she would be calm and composed, in fact, the polished, perfect sloth.

We were right, for now, whenever one of us passes under the cacao-tree, which is her favourite resting place, a little face looks down, pleading to be carried. Once in your arms, she snuggles down with every sign of pleasure and closes her eyes. She cuddles up to you, her little head pressed against your chest, as though listening to the beat of your heart and the rhythm of your breathing. Perhaps memories of childhood have stirred within her. She certainly likes to be cradled and sung to sleep with a lullaby ust as any child might.

The marriage took place and cuffing and hair-pulling became things of the past. Our two a-is now devoted their waking hours to the delights of *dolce far niente*, punctuated by long periods of sleep.

After the effort of eating, they always have to have a snooze, for which they go to the sloping part of the garden and there select a stump or root to clasp—sloths must have something in their arms for their happiness to be complete. Later in the afternoon, after another snack, they repair to their true habitat, the shaded foliage of the trees, and there we can always find them, two grey woolly bundles, hanging from a branch, sound asleep, or perhaps squatting side by side in perfect concord, and there they will stay without moving all through the night and well into the morning. The only creatures that can disturb them are red Azteca ants, which live in their myriads in the hollow trunks of the ymbahuba trees. Their bite is rather painful and I once watched Nepomuk's reactions when some of these ants crawled into one of his nostrils when he was asleep. After a considerable interval, he raised a paw to brush the intruders away, but by that time the ants were well inside. After a further interval for reflection, he must have reached the conclusion that these creatures were his enemies, for he adopted the sloth's threatening attitude: one arm drawn well back with its three sharp daggers ready to strike. At what, I wondered, was the blow going to be aimed—at his own nose? The arm remained thus poised for a long time, while (or so it seemed) the penny slowly, slowly, dropped. Then, the threatening arm gently and resignedly sank to Nepomuk's side, and his face took on a bewildered expression.

Once asleep for the night, movement would not return to him until the sun was high in the heavens and the air heavy with the scent of maracuja blossom, then he would wake, blink at the bright day, yawn and take a leisurely stroll through the trees.

Unless captive and asleep in its mother's arms, the baby sloth clung
with wide-straddled legs to its mother's belly

All but invisible in her mother's fur

Her venturesomeness stopped at water which she would only cross on her parent's back

Maya reads to the sloths

The baby sloth starts to climb but gets into difficulties

Mother and daughter hanging from a mulungu tree

Our two a-is throve in the freedom of our garden-wilderness until one day we noticed that the female seemed a bit off colour; instead of sunning herself in the banana tree or near the white-flowering myrtle, she went off to a shady corner where she sat and dozed, with an enigmatic smile on her face. We were rather worried in case she might be sickening for some illness, but comforted ourselves with the knowledge that she was eating, and sleeping, enough for two, and this was indeed the truth, for not long afterwards our five-year-old daughter, Maya, discovered a baby sloth peeping out of its mother's fur.

Its eyes were open but its eyebrows not yet white, and its body, except for its pink tummy, which needed no covering since it was always pressed close to mother, was covered in fluff.

When we were able to examine it we found that it weighed just over seven and a half ounces, about a twentieth of what its adult weight would be, which by comparison with other baby mammals is very little.

Probably the little sloth had arrived in the early morning when the jaguar has gone to bed, for females give birth on the ground; after which they remove all trace of the event by swallowing the afterbirth; then they take to the trees with the baby clinging on to their fur.

Mother sloths do very little for their offspring except provide them with milk and a back to lean on. Our baby sloth clung with wide-straddled legs to the mother's belly and she stayed still and was all but invisible. When the mother was climbing a tree with a thin trunk which she could clasp between the soles of her feet and her claws, then the baby was all right because its mother's body would not be actually touching the trunk. But, if the tree they were going up was a really big and high one—and Nepomuk's wife was nothing if not ambitious —then things became dangerous, for, if the baby were to avoid being scraped off by cross branches, it had to squeeze as close to mother's body as it could to pass underneath the obstacle—even this did not always work and sometimes it had to leave its safe position and dart up on to one of its mother's flanks. It rarely went on to mother's back, presumably because it was unable to suckle from there. In the pursuit of food, mother sloth never showed any consideration for her offspring, and climbed about as if the baby were not there. The real test of the little sloth's agility came when its mother insisted on squeezing between two branches, for then it had to climb on to and over the obstacle and on emerging land on the lower part of its mother's body and then climb back to its former position. We were relieved to find that even at a week old, the baby sloth was able to deal with any situation into which its thoughtless parent took it. This was partly due to the fact that, at that age, there is nothing slothful about a sloth. It can jump about its mother like a flea and appears to be made of rubber.

Paternal affection is not part of the male sloth's make-up and Nepomuk paid no attention to his child, even when I presented it to him. Its upbringing was left entirely to its mother and to us.

Knowing that the ymbahuba is the sloth's favourite food, we planted an additional three dozen in our garden for the benefit of mother and child and felt that we had done them proud, for both buds and fan-shaped leaves are edible. But as soon as the baby began to suckle, the mother sloth would eat nothing but the juicy top-shoots, of which each tree has only one. In consequence, we found it very difficult to provide her with an adequate supply.

The Latin name for a sloth is *tardipes*, slow-foot, the French call it *paresseux*, but the Spaniards, evidently thinking of the babies, called it *perico ligero*, nimble Peter, and nimble our young sloth certainly was. Having seen it snuggling up in its mother's fur, we tried to cuddle it —forgetting that the skin of a mother sloth is as tough as an old boot and that the clasp of those needle-sharp claws which, though tiny, are immensely strong, is excruciating. I can speak of this from experience, so can my wife who reluctantly agreed to hold the little sloth while I photographed it.

The appearance of the baby a-i changed very quickly. Her (for now we saw that she was a female) high fore-head became lower, her little black nose grew more pointed and her bright eyes more artful. Maya started calling it her 'little hedgehog' and certainly she was rather like an urchin.

So long as she had her mother's fur to hide in, she allowed herself the quick movements which the adult sloth does not indulge in. If anything frightened her, she struck out wildly, her little arms going like flails, hitting out in every direction.

Some racial memory, perhaps of their arch-enemy, the jaguar, makes all sloths, the babies as well as the adults, bury their droppings. On the first occasion or two, the baby sloth duly performed this ritual in her mother's fur. The signal of what is about to happen is given by the tail, so, if you have a sloth on your lap and see its small tail make excavating movements, put it down very quickly for it is incredible how much such a little creature can excrete, but then it only defecates every seven or eight days. Afterwards there is a distinct difference in girth and this fact, no doubt, gave rise to the legend that a sloth leaving a tree, full-fed and fat, by the time it has managed to crawl across to another and climb into it, will be thin. In its natural state a sloth seldom comes down to the ground except for the purpose of burying its droppings, which it cannot let fall from the tree without betraying its presence.

At three months the baby sloth tipped the scales at nineteen and a quarter ounces and evidently thought the time had come to practise climbing on her own. I watched her start up her first tree, for three feet she climbed quite quickly, though somewhat hampered by her little pot belly, then suddenly she seemed to feel giddy, stopped and obviously wanted to climb down again, but discovered that she could not get into reverse. Dismayed, she clung to the trunk, trembling, and gave a desperate *ah-eee* (an octave higher than her mother's call). This woke her mother, who yawned and looked round anxiously, turned her head more than a full revolution in an upward spiral, raised a long arm and pointed it in the direction from which the distress signals were coming. Fortunately the rescuing arm was within the baby's reach. She seized on to it and used it as a bridge to return to her parent.

Maya was always worried in case the sloths were too hot in their furry coats, so one day I showed her a sloth's hair through my microscope. They have ribbon-shaped covers which look like elder pith. It is this pithy covering that protects the a-i from extremes of heat and cold, the young sloths acquire it at the age of about a year.

On the outside, one can often see a hint of green, this is algae growing on the hairs as lichen grows on trees; sometimes moths too will take up residence in a sloth's fur.

Normally, the sloth is a very silent creature. Its doleful *ah-ee* is seldom heard and the only other sound it makes is when, at certain seasons of the year, love impels it to call for a mate, then as it sits on a branch it emits a loud bird-like *eee* or *a-eee* at regular intervals.

When full-fed and snuggled in the hollow of one's arm, our young a-i would grind her teeth in pleasure, as her father does during his Sunday nap, making a throaty and only just audible sound, but one which there is no mistaking.

It was obviously going to be a long time before there was anything slothful about the new member of our family, for she was always on the move and, like all babies, she imitated her elders and betters. If one of her parents brandished an arm in the sloth's gesture of warning and defiance, the baby would do the same, employing both arms and often a leg as well. Sometimes her mother decided that even she had had enough of her daughter's pranks and that the situation called for chastisement, preferably a box on the ear. The blow, well-aimed and deliberate, would have reached its mark, if the intended recipient had been a year or two older, but the infant was always well out of reach before the maternal paw was halfway towards her; as a result the blow would often land on the mother's belly.

As the weeks passed, the little sloth became more venturesome and when her mother was climbing, would jump off her and go experimenting on her own. The mother sloth was invariably sure that such behaviour was dangerous and stretched out a helping arm, but this only infuriated the baby who drummed on it with her fists in a regular tantrum. Afterwards there would be a lengthy pause, followed by two deep sighs, while the mother considered the situation. Then she would seize the struggling and furious small sloth by the scruff and replace her on her tummy. Such an exertion caused the mother sloth to fall asleep and a few moments later, the baby would be off again into the nearest red-blossomed mulungu.

You might expect any young animal to gambol or play, but neither Nepomuk nor his wife ever did so. He became sedate very early in life and even his daughter, when she was still lively, never really played.

However, her horizon was expanding daily as she explored farther and farther afield—to the white cotton-plants, the yellow stems of the bamboo thicket, the aerial roots of the matapau, the blossoming palisander, and she even went as far as the crest of the patchy grey massaranduba. Nor was her exploration confined to the garden, she investigated the house, and she climbed up and over everything. Her greatest achievement, perhaps, and one that will be long remembered, was her solo ascent—without any equipment—of the sheer east wall of the bathroom. For steepness, smoothness and exposure, the famous Eiger or Matterhorn faces pale in comparison with our tiles.

Though she had become more and more daring and independent, there was one sphere in which she remained a baby; she would not venture into water alone and if water had to be crossed, she would do so riding on her mother's back.

The world must be a confusing and sometimes a

frightening place for a small sloth. Even the pink paina bush, which was a favourite haunt of the little sloth, provided her with such shocks that more than once she almost tumbled out of it. The first time this happened was when what appeared to be one of the long stamens of one of its brightly coloured flowers proved to be the arm of a robber-spider lurking in the chalice. On another occasion, she was investigating what looked like a delicious leaf on a branch of nhangapirih, when it suddenly darted away in front of her nose; and there were times when a piece of dry wood suddenly came to life and proved to be a staff grasshopper, the largest insect in the world—and rather awe-inspiring.

The months passed and the myrtle was in flower again. It was a year since our young sloth had been born. She had now acquired an adult coat and no longer needed her mother's care. She weighed thirty ounces. Although she would not be fully adult till she was six years old, she was extending her area of operations, going as far as the no-man's-land between garden and forest. It was obvious that it would not be long before she would be off and away, perhaps never to return. If she wanted to go, she must do so. We had no right to try and stop her. We could only hope that she would pay us visits.

Perhaps she will, and in any case we can count on Nepomuk and his wife remaining with us.

THE END